Morning Grace

Julia Cook

Morning Grace by Julia Cook

Email: hello@orenaugmountainpublishing.com
Website: www.orenaugmountainpublishing.com

ISBN: 979-8-9925369-8-0

For
Patrick, who always has my back
Vanessa and Ryan, who opened my heart
Jade, Tai and Brady, who remind me of who I really am

Morning Grace

Table of Contents

Introduction

When I wrote the poems in this collection during the last few years, I had no thought of organized categories, but simply wrote what moved me at the time. As I reviewed the poems, I realized many of them were about family, and others seemed to organize themselves into like groups.

In the same way that a photographer might visit a scenic place many times in different seasons and conditions, I return to the same themes, approaching them from various perspectives. These poems are arranged in five sections: Origins, Family, Nature & Life, Women, and Spirit.

It is my hope that readers will find words within these pages that illuminate the grace found within, and all around, us.

I
Origins

American Dreams

For Mary Flaherty,
first generation to leave
the land of pestilence and death,
the dream appeared as
mounds of wholesome food:
potatoes, parsnips, lamb stew
with barley and cabbage;
food lining the streets and
straining the cupboards,
plenty for everyone
with leftovers to spare.

She knit a small circle of yarn,
held out her hands,
and there was food, hard-earned.
Hunger sometimes, but never like before.

She passed the knit work to Bridget,
her daughter, who held it in her hands,
worked it into something grander.
Could it be...
a home, a place to raise these twenty children,
a steady job for Michael,
a real place in the safe center of things,
away from the craggy edges?

The child, Julia, watched
her mother work the knitting,
added her own scraps of yarn
to the growing piece.
Later, she wore it like a shawl
on the day her boardinghouse
opened for business,
a substantial garment,
large enough to cover
daughters, son, brothers,

sisters, Mam, and Pap
under its shelter.

In time, she bought houses on the hill
to hold four of her daughters,
each woman cradling her own dream.

In one house,
Evangeline opens her mother's trunk.
She removes waves of woven yarn,
speckled brown, yellow, red, green,
wraps herself in their soft folds.
Across the room,
I wait in the wing chair,
wait for my grandmother
to come and enfold me
in our river of dreams.

Song for the Ancestors

A circle of women, each in her illuminated screen-square,
come together to listen, to sing, to shore up one another's hearts.
The day is November 1, Samhain in the Celtic calendar,
a day for remembering our dead, for honoring our ancestors,

a time to listen keenly to their stories, their songs.
The veil between the living and the dead is thin today;
we reach out to receive them. We sing our given names
and the names of those who came before us,

grateful to know and to be known.
We listen to a newborn song one of us has made—
about time passing, the awareness that our stay here is brief,
about making that time count, being a blessing here
and beyond.

We listen to a softened, slowed-down version of "Both Sides Now"—
how the message ripens and deepens with the change—
then we sing "Saints Go Marching In"—unhurried—
the sweetness of our voices lingering on each phrase,

becoming soulful, wide and full. The *saints go marching*,
the saints go dancing, they hold hands with us and we whirl together
in this narrow span, hearts radiating a poignant joy,
filling heaven and earth with our persistent light.

Origin

Fairies whisper to the barefoot girl, *Come to the garden, come.*
She skitters past the boogeyman's shed, through the wooden gate
where a peach tree waits. Traipsing through uncut grass,
she nestles beneath her grandfather's fruit-laden tree.
Birds sing an overheard Italian song: *Danza! Chikka, chikka, danza!*—
and she spins and wheels beneath shimmering curled leaves.
A wind enrapts her high above the tree's crown
for a breathless view of neighboring countries
with carefully tended plots of tomato, eggplant, zucchini,
wafting scents of fresh bread, roasted peppers, onions with garlic and olive oil.
Honeysuckle vines beribbon and caress her, cascading down
to their point of origin in the rich soil; even deeper,
feathery roots mingle with those of the blackberry bush
and the peach tree, and the girl.
There's a trace of salt in the air and his voice in her ear,
Come to the garden, bambina, come.

Becoming

On a virginal spring day I walked down Hart Street
toward my piano teacher's English Tudor home
with Leroy Anderson's "The First Day of Spring"
floating through my mind's ear—
matching the day, as music often does.
Its melody climbed up a small hill,
lush with daffodils and hyacinths, note-by-note,
until reaching the summit, then looked down
over all of my 14 years. I breathed in newborn air
and it merged with rogue energy rising in my body,
unrecognizable yet faintly familiar. Harmonic overtones
enlivened the early green sprout unfurling in my belly
...vague stirrings... yearnings...
I was different, I could finally admit;
I was metamorphosing into some new creature,
and that was exciting—and terrifying. As the music
swelled up and down softly rounded verdant hills,
I followed, choiceless; beauty and music mingled
with pain, everything so close, so present.
I allowed myself to feel all of it. When I arrived
at my piano teacher's house, my circumference
wide as the orbiting moon, I wondered
how I would fit inside the doorway.

Shop of Remembrance

This secondhand shop, teeming with memories,
A hodgepodge of silver tea sets and vintage china.
I feel the pull of nostalgia rise up inside me,
Reaching out to times long past.

A hodgepodge of silver tea sets and vintage china.
I remember when grace and order eased our days.
Reaching out to times long past,
I see my mother on Thanksgiving Day.

I remember when grace and order eased our days.
She set the good silverware on a lace tablecloth.
I see my mother on Thanksgiving Day
Showing her love and care in small gestures.

As she sets the good silverware on a lace tablecloth,
I feel the pull of nostalgia rise up inside me.
She showed her love and care in small gestures.
This secondhand shop, teeming with memories.

Honored Place

This table full of pretty china
Silver moon dessert plates,
eggshell Nautilus saucers, teacups
edged with petite flowers of mauve, pink and gold,
an assortment of mismatched flea market finds.

Treasured wedding gifts from long ago,
they graced family tables on holidays and birthdays,
their beauty and charm like the familiar faces
you could count on being there year after year.

Now, separated from their totality, like families
broken and scattered after a matriarch's death,
here they sit, exquisite relics of an earlier time,
still beguiling, beckoning to be used, admired,

cared for, despite a few chips and crazings;
to be set gently in a place of honor
as their owner once was, to be seen
for whom they really are—elegant, old,
cherishable treasures.

Uncle Al's Farm in June

My sister and I, freed from the city,
live long days under a wide endless sky,
hot sun on shoulders, cool shade beneath pines,
skipping stones over the sheen of a still pond,

then sitting in long grass by the water,
bedazzled by dancing light on its surface.
Unknown birds circle and call out our names
as we conjure a life here beyond summer,

beyond everything we'd known in neighborhoods
of three-family houses and paved sidewalks,
timed schedules of school, play, and sleep.
A good life—but wouldn't this be better?

Nature's rhythms hold us, gentle and free,
planting seeds of new ways to feel and be.

Margaret's Table

My mother's table held sustenance for a family of four,
holiday hams and turkeys for the whole clan,
birthday cakes to celebrate our progress and growth.

My mother's table held cups of tea
with fresh banana bread and homemade hermits
to share with her three sisters,
while weaving the threads of their lives
in ever stronger bonds.

My mother's table held poster board, markers, and pencils
for the art projects of her two girls,
the ephemera of communal craft-making
as we three fashioned bird cages
and topiary trees for family showers.

My mother's table held us close to its perimeter
as we ate our morning grapefruit and Cheerios,
tomato soup and grilled cheese sandwiches
for school-day lunches—and for supper,
fragrant Italian dishes learned from her mother-in-law.

My mother's table held the vibrations
of laughter, game playing, and fun
from the generations who gathered there.

My mother's table held the tension of an unwanted change,
the absence of a father, the addition of a new man in the family.

My mother's table held kindness and compassion
as my sister and I kept her company over jigsaw puzzles
and coloring books while she drifted into a
shadowed, compromised perception of the world.

Now, my mother's table holds us still, in the dining room of my home.
I wipe its smooth surface, remembering the care she gave it,
and the care she gave to us.
This simple table has seen much, knows much,
a silent witness to our ways of being together.
As we sit shoulder to shoulder around its familiar curves,
I imagine the good energy
absorbed by this sturdy maple servant.
It emanates and caresses us with warm, grounded comfort,
connecting all who gather here.

Back Then

Smoothing lavender lotion on my arms
I am surprised by the deep purple bruise
from yesterday
when a technician expertly siphoned
two vials of blood from my body
and bandaged the spot,
advising me to apply pressure unless
I wanted an ugly bruise to appear.

Yet here it is, a purple blotch
with faint yellow undertones
gracing the inside of my arm
like a badly done tattoo of a dying Iris.

It reminds me of the scabs of my childhood—
war wounds on elbows and knees
caused by the sidewalk rising up
to smack me as I ran for the Good Humor truck
or the ground suddenly heaving like the ocean
throwing me down, bicycle and all.

Every kid had them, reddish-brown points of pride
we compared while recounting exactly
how it happened, after hiccupped crying
and sting of Mercurochrome faded from memory.

Now I hear stories of accidents and operations
told by friends, sometimes with great relish and detail,
other times in matter-of-fact reports.
There's awareness of pending physical ailments
as we age, and the desire to rebound quickly,
to live as fully as we can for as long as we can.
To laugh with friends, walk in quiet woods,
witness a chorus of migrating geese
and be freshened by joy.

Simple happiness and resilience
like back then, when we picked up our bikes,
strapped on our roller skates, and with eager shouts
took fearlessly to the streets once again.

Information, Please

In the den of my childhood home sat a chair,
big and square with wide flat arms, a good place
to bury myself in a new book from the Weekly Reader Book Club.
There was room for my sister and I to unfold our cardboard Barbie homes,
to reveal patterned floor, sturdy cardboard furniture,
built-in closet and make-up table.
My brunette Barbie was a stewardess and hers a blonde nurse
who both had an active social life, going out nightly in custom gowns
painstakingly sewn by our mother.

One day as Mom rummaged in the den closet, I begged her
to tell me what the word scrawled on a downtown wall meant.
It began with the letter "F" and held a potent, dangerous energy,
but she refused to say. She bought volumes of The Golden Book Encyclopedia
at the supermarket, one each week, until we had a complete set.
There was a lot of information in there, but certain things
were not mentioned.
Like how babies got inside Aunt Bette, and how, a while later, a new cousin
arrived.

I remember when she sat me down on the sofa and explained that sex
was like putting a key in a keyhole, planting a seed.
I hadn't imagined this arrangement, and found it both interesting
and embarrassing. I added this information to the cryptic comment
made by Sister Josephine when she warned us girls
that "an hour of pleasure could lead to a lifetime of pain".

Later, in the privacy of the locker room, we were giddy.
It took one hour!
Now that was information we could use.

Lovesong

"Our Love is Here to Stay"
Ira wrote the words.
He married them utterly to
George's simple melody.

"The more I read the papers,
the less I comprehend."
The headline said
George was gone,

yet the telephone
still rang, movies played,
the radio clicked on
with its usual static.

The worst disaster had
happened, worse than
mountains crumbling
or Gibraltar tipping into the

sea, but one shining fact
remained; George and Ira
were brothers still; their
love would never go away.

My father played his version,
"My Love is Here to Stay"
love is mine, not yours or ours,
don't go away.

But my mother didn't listen;
she had to go. Even so,
I still see Dad and I
sitting on the piano bench

playing and singing that song,
his favorite,
strung together by a glowing
filament that, once begun

could never blink out.
The scene lights up
in memory,
replete with the feel

of cool piano keys,
softly struck,
our closeness,
the exquisite melody

and words, so perfect
together, as we were
in that moment.
Two slim, fearful souls

lit up from within
by the power of
the Gershwins'
indirect current

engulfing us
in streams of love,
pure and clear.
Here to stay.

II
Family

At Nick's Corner Cafe

our four-top is an island
in a swirl of sound and motion.
The no-nonsense waitress
takes orders, hoists trays,
plates up tables like dealing cards.
Fish and chips, Monte Christos,
steaming French onion soup
delivered to families, grey-haired
couples, women in lively conversation.

We four share vacation photos,
swap family stories, reminisce,
catch up, toss out future plans.
A rude crash of dishes in the bin
and my partner startles—
it's not his kind of place,
the pop and crackle of life
at full volume and up close.
My auntie, from a big family, is unbothered.
She got through her five-kids-in-a-row long ago.
Next table, two angel-faced babies
eating ziti with their fingers can't keep their eyes
off her as she chats with them
like a resident grandma.

Then it hits me—
this is a family dining room
like the one in my great grandma's boardinghouse
where strangers gathered round the table for meals
and made a family of themselves.
We may not know each other at Nick's,
but we come for the same reasons—
for warmth and sustenance
in a place where we can be
who we are, unadorned,
where we can look at one another

and recognize ourselves
on a cold Friday noon in February.
If you look beyond the coffee, bacon,
babble, cries, and clash of cutlery, you might
perceive a makeshift family of sorts,
presided over by an edgy waitress
and a short order cook (never seen)
who hold open this welcoming space
like blood relatives.

Walnut Hill, New Britain, Connecticut

In June at the top of Walnut Hill Park you come
to a wide circle of roses in every color and variety—
gold, ruby, peach-colored faces staring up at the sun.
Heady perfume scents the air as you gaze
at the central pool, cooling your senses
in the fountain spray.
In this place mom and her sisters
splashed and played on hot summer days;
in winter it was their skating rink.
One sister's wedding photos were taken
here among the blooming roses.
From this place you can glimpse
the hospital where they were born,
where my daughter and I were born.
On these rolling hills I roamed the lawns
with my first real boyfriend, following the path
to the art museum, a sanctuary from teenage troubles.
A short stroll leads you to the music shell
where our family sat on blankets, thrilled to hear
Dad play with his band on warm summer nights.
On the same stage, high school already a memory,
our graduating class stepped up to collect their diplomas.

Though I no longer live in this city, I return to the hill
with my child and grandchild, point out sites of our heritage.
"How did I miss this?" my daughter asks. Somehow among visits
to her grandmother, Polish grocery, art museum, I forgot
to include this jewel of a park. I remember the day she was born,
the brilliance of October foliage beckoning. We parked the car
and contractions promptly stopped. I proposed a walk in the park;
my husband took my arm, firmly directing me toward the hospital.
Now, a lifetime later, he points to a window in the building,
tells our daughter that's where she was born.
I smile at my grandson,
circle complete.

Cooking With Brady

Age 5—Get some apples, cut slices with your plastic chef knife,
then chop the fruit into chunky blocks. Gather into a bowl.
Do the same with bananas, pears, and cheese. Bring everything
to the blanket-fort in the living room for a picnic.
Let grandma eat most of it.

Age 6—Look around the kitchen for some sweet potatoes.
Scrub them hard and long, poke holes, place in the microwave.
Maybe they'll explode like last time! If not, take them out—
hot! hot!—Slice each in half and let the steam rise.
Try to wait until they cool. Get tired of waiting and peel off the skin—
ouch! ouch!—Dice and eat the yummy insides.

Age 7—Take a ripe mango, lop off a slice with grandma's sharp knife—
careful! Cut tic-tac-toe lines into the yellow flesh,
bend back the skin and chop off the little cubes. So cool!

Age 8 & 9—Shape soft dough into bagels, bread, pizza.
Breathe in the bakery aroma of the kitchen. When done,
go get grandpa to view the masterpieces, then slice and share.

Age 10—Measure ingredients for oatmeal chocolate chip cookies,
licking coconut sugar off your fingers as often as possible.
Mix it all together, then let grandma plop them on the sheet
and into the oven (the boring parts). Wait and wait till
the kitchen smells like vanilla, sugar, and chocolate.
That's when you know they're almost done.

Let the cookies cool for about 10 seconds, then eat them hot,
chocolate melting on fingers. Drink a tall glass of cold milk,
then eat *just one more cookie* 10 times.
Remember to bring home the leftovers!

To a Beloved Seventeen-Year-Old Boy

For Tai

Spending a few days with you
has been like a ride in the funhouse—
and I mean that in the best possible way.

That moment of pleasant surprise when you decided
to learn how to play "Jingle Bell Rock" on the piano
then worked your way up to "Pachelbel's Canon"
and "Fur Elise" (first section) in the space of a day.

I had my doubts but you insisted, politely refusing
my offer of simpler versions. Your absorption
and persistence were admirable, especially for one
who had never before played the instrument,

and it led me to remember when you were nine
and refused to continue with public school,
even then practicing those qualities
of determination and devotion to doing things your way.

Still, I couldn't help but remind you that my students
always start with simple arrangements
so they can feel successful, but
since you are not my student, you ignored this

and instead asked questions about notation and keys
as I marveled at your unspoiled confidence,
your meticulous parsing of notes and phrases
until you had mastered the measures.

After the rest of the house had retired to bed,
you kept late hours, warmed by the crackling fire
as perhaps Beethoven was when he composed
that ubiquitous piece, and Grieg could not have

been more focused than you as your fingers
explored the depths of the Mountain King,
or Debussy when he transposed the
light of the moon into ethereal sound

and I suppose the light beaming from your hands
was no surprise as you played into the night
cocooned in the shelter of your innate knowing,
while outside the winter wind danced and hummed along.

She Sleeps

For Jade

The slender young woman
on my sofa,
one hand cradles her cheek,
the other lies gently at her neck.
Her long legs nest together
like bird wings.
Her face,
surrounded by a splayed halo
of flaxen hair
resides in perfect stillness,
the visage of a dreamer
traversing a universe
of places, people, possibilities
she may not recall
in her waking state.

Gazing in the half light
I see her younger self rise up,
turn to me with
a mischievous grin
then race through the house
dark curls flying
laughter and joy spilling
everywhere
as memories flood
my brain and heart...
the two of us on the porch swing
inventing silly songs and
secret picnics under a blanket fort
and laughing till our sides ache
from telling tall tales.

She doesn't remember those details.
In her race to adulthood
scenes have blurred and faded;
only a few clear images remain
because growing up is hard, and
sometimes we discard the best parts.

So I keep them for her—
this sleeping two-decades-old beauty.
I hold these memories safe
for her to find and remember.

Ronnie

The way my cousin Ronnie once
caressed a vase with a dust cloth,
polishing each curve with the
focus and attention of a monk
repeating the circular motion of
one prayer
over and over until the light shines through.

Like a mother, loving her child
day after day,
constantly aware of the
luminous being within,
her warm palms smoothing brow,
cheeks, back, shoulders...
Even when the glass darkens
obscuring the throb of light within,
she never stops polishing, polishing...

Ronnie patiently rubs the vase.
In a nearby bedroom,
his once-robust mother,
skin wrapped over bones,
lies dying.
Her losses litter the floor
like piles of discarded clothing.
What remains, the steady flame
of her generous heart,
has become a wildfire
threatening to consume
her entire being.

By the fireplace,
Ronnie traces
the contours of the vase,
worries it so thin
that it vanishes...
and he is left
holding pure light
in his bare hands.

Felicia

You're the cousin we admired, bright-smiling, blonde hair
in a perfect flip, centered in the photo
with brown-haired me and my sister on either side.
Oh, those holidays at your parents' wonderland of a home!
Easter evenings before the magic television, waiting to witness
Dorothy's transformation as she stepped from her
gray-toned world into the brilliant chroma of Oz.
Remember those days
when we'd join hands and slowly
ring-around-the-rosy for my dad's home movies?
And those years
sitting on your bed, silly and free,
listening to Beach Boys albums
as you dispensed makeup and hair wisdom.
No hint of your rational future as a registered nurse
or the rushing years of juggling job, husband, children.
You learned to be strong and soft as a willow tree.

Now, so many years later, we three gaze
at each others' mutually blue eyes, the one part
that never really changed.
You still possess your signature smile
beneath sleek hair, white and fine
and your face displays
a galaxy of experiences.
The cadence of your words,
so like your mother's—
unhurried—offers space
for us to bathe in the waters of reminiscence
until the current brings us back to
now, now, now,
our work, our passions, children, and grandchildren.
The bond among us solid and holding
as we were once held,
a bright constellation of family
shining into the future.

Dream

For my cousin Gary

Black-haired cousin, you come to call,
with a Chinese black lacquer painting.
We sit close on your mother's soft couch
like lovers reunited.

With a Chinese black lacquer painting
you show your clarity and vision,
like lovers reunited
in familiar embrace.

I show my clarity and vision
when your mother appears, young and whole.
In familiar embrace
I hold her in my arms.

When your mother appears, young and whole,
she wears spinning gossamer.
I hold her in my arms
as her light pours into me.

She wears spinning gossamer.
We sit close on your mother's soft couch
as her light pours into us.
Black-haired cousin, you come to call.

Cookie's Way

For my father-in-law, Edward Latham Cook

He was an unassuming man,
a cigar chomper,
not much of a talker.
Never planned on having
such a big, unruly family,
strong-willed wife,
and kids who
didn't always get the importance
of doing your job well,
the cardinal rule
he'd lived by since boyhood,
a rule that served him well
at MIT, in the ROTC, and in his work
as mechanical engineer.

In '42, it was back to the Army,
training in Ordnance School,
1st Lieutenant in charge of
supplies and vehicles
on the home front, and later,
field artillery in Rhineland and Ardennes.
Working at battlefield's edge
who can say what else his duties required?
He returned home with a collection
of Nazi badges, pins, and buttons
along with a Mauser rifle
and pair of bayonets.

Back at his job in a small
Illinois town, he met her—
lovely, young, two kids already
and never yet been treated right.
He opened his heart
thinking how he could save her

and she would rescue him
from loneliness.

They tried, through two more kids,
crises, illness, expectations,
arguments. She wanted him
to be everything—fair,wise father,
strong, romantic husband.
He did his job, went to work,
supported them the way he knew.
Never spoke of the war years,
what he'd seen and done. Even at
the annual reunion of his Unit,
they never spoke of it, only caught up
with news of births, promotions,
graduations. It was comforting
to be among men who remembered
what he would never forget.

When the time came,
his passing was a blessing—
so much had been lost.
At the military graveside service,
National Reserve soldiers
in dress blues executed
a three-gun salute with precision;
then the mournful notes of "Taps"
pierced the air, igniting
the family's grief.
Silence wrapped its arms
around them as two soldiers
unfolded the flag in well-practiced ritual,
then refolded
triangle upon triangle
into a neat wedge
carried with dignity
to the eldest son, on behalf of
"a grateful nation
as a symbol of our appreciation

for your loved one's honorable
and faithful service."
For Edward, Ed, Cookie.
His family felt the loss of all he was
and all he could have been,
but no one could argue that he hadn't always
completed the work he'd set out to do
in his own way
and that he'd done the job well.

How I Met Your Father

It was in Switzerland, on the shore of Lake Geneva
where I looked down and saw what appeared to be
a worn piece of soap. I picked it up to discover
a bone-colored stone
with three rounded sides and slightly gritty texture
and slipped it in my pocket
to serve as talisman for the rest of the trip.

I walked along the shore with a tall, dark-haired boy
from our group, feeding swans, joking and parrying
the afternoon away. Next day, we sat together in the back seat
of a rented Renault as the teacher in charge drove us
to the city of Bern to explore,
but
soon his injured ankle flared and we were sent to fetch the car,
finally found it
then drove through a labyrinth of streets for an hour
never once spotting the corner where the teacher waited.

We decided to make our way back to the hotel in Montreux,
consulting maps, asking directions of people who spoke
only German. The afternoon dimmed to twilight,
then inky black, as we drove on twisting alpine roads
until after midnight, frustration and fear rising.
We pulled over near a huddled group of cows
and I touched the stone in my pocket as we got out
to stretch under the vast onyx sky set with
staring moon and scatter of stars.

When we finally made it back to the hotel at 3 AM,
the teacher appeared in the hallway in his night shirt,
red-faced and livid.
We slept right through the departure
for the day's excursion, and instead rented bikes,
riding to Château de Chillon, the place Lord Byron
immortalized in his Prisoner poem. The two of us

breezed through cold stone hallways, bare rooms
and prison cells like children released from school.

On the way back, we stopped for chocolat chaud and escargot.
Throughout the day the soapstone
lay in my pocket where my fingers often sought
and held it, a warming presence,
fitting my hand perfectly.

Morning Grace

I eat and read in the quiet morning,
muesli with walnuts and almond milk
blueberries floating on top.
Only the occasional bird call
or hum of a distant car
accompanies my progress
to the bottom of the bowl
where I slurp each spoonful noisily
(feeling slightly wicked)—
it's something I would never do
if you were here
though *you've* been known to do it
and I've never said a word.
Not. One. Word.
(Poison glances don't count.)

But ah, the freedom of early morning,
listening to the duet of the mourning dove's
coo against my noisy slurping
as you lie in bed
ignorant of my
cave woman manners,
a guilty exception to
my usual impeccable grace
that has never wavered in our
fifty long years of marriage.

Well, perhaps a teensy bit,
but I doubt it.
I doubt it very much.

Sometimes I Forget Completely

Sometimes I forget completely
who I am.
I run around
here and there.
I talk too much.
I treat you like a stranger.
I allow a build-up of plaque
to form around my heart.
A roboton
with the appearance of meaning.

I forget completely sometimes
that the mere fact of you
is a miracle
    that your everyday offerings:
    to pick up a movie and Hunan Shrimp
    change the oil, stack the logs
    free my shoulders of their knots
are gifts of love, not penances
you owe me.

I forget that once
all you had to do was
look at me—one look
and you entered
my bones, my heart, my toes.
I took you in completely.

I forget sometimes
that I need the
oxygen of love to live.
I forget to breathe.
    I forget who you are.
     I forget
       sometimes
          completely.

Spanning the Gap

There are bridges that lead to nowhere
and bridges that span the gap over
a stream, a river, or part of an ocean
carrying us safely to the other side.

And there's the bridge of a song that deftly
escorts us from Part A to the deeper terrain
of Part B where we learn why a heart hesitates
or is breaking with the stress of loving you
before we return to the safe shore of home.

And what about the bridges I have built to get to you:
the fragile rope connector that swings
over a deep canyon, holding the weight
of my careful steps as you wait on the other side,

or the one made of brittle twigs snapping smartly
under my foot falls, and the sturdy one made of iron
scorching hot under the bright sun—but it's

the single filament cast over a river
like the dancing line of a fly fisherman
that snags your attention with its careless beauty,
latches onto your heart and finally
brings you home to me.

Interbeing

It was a Friday morning.
My mother lay laboring
to give birth to herself,
breath even, steady, purposeful.

I held her hand
as no one did when
she labored for me,
her body doing what it knew
how to do, even in twilight sleep.

Now she lay still and sunken,
eyes nearly closed, focused
in some other consciousness.
Nothing left but the persistent see-saw
of her breath.

When a woman gives birth
there is a point of transition—
contractions become intense,
close together—
a sign the baby will soon be born.

I watched my mother for a sign
but, hour after hour,
only her focused delicate breathwork.
Like when she bent over an intricate
sewing project, she would persevere
until the end.

Was it a sign? In the afternoon, her breath
became lighter, less audible,
yet regular as her marching gait
when we walked downtown
to buy dishtowels, dresses, and nonpareils.

At 5:49, her ethereal breath
vanished without ceremony.
It slipped from the room,
leaving a white stillness
that flowed to every corner.

We gathered closer around her.
A rising cloud of peace
enveloped us and we inhaled
its comforting scent.
It filled us deep and wide with love,
expanding outward to include

All that had been
All that would be

You Are Here

You are here now in visible light.
I see your body's topography,
feel its yielding warmth.
Your whispers and declarations
reflect a wheel of spinning emotions,
one melting into the next,
your unique song.

You are here, in my mind,
a million impressions
made over the years,
the color of my memories
matching yours, mostly,
our ways of being
synchronized
by familiarity and routine—
except for those private pockets kept
for what is yours alone, and what is mine.

You are here, in my heart,
a permanent resident
tethered by joy, sorrow,
tenderness, anger
so that even when you're absent
for an hour, a day, or a week,
even in that spaciousness
you are here.

So if you should transform before I do,
I wonder—will your presence remain,
reassuring and supporting as always?
Will I love you as much or more
when you are invisible light?

III
Nature and Life

At Hollow Park

Late summer among the trees,
the sun lights up heart-shaped foliage
of a grey birch. I touch their leaf tips,
weathered by the season, transformed
from rosy buds to delicate green newborns
to adolescents waving lusty flags in the heat of July.

Now, compromised by nibbling squirrels,
some hang like tattered curtains.
Even so, sturdy trunk and branches support
the whole congregation as they shimmer
and sing their hushed hymn,
and below, a genealogy of roots
spreads and wanders.

We stand side by side, two seasoned sojourners,
taking in sounds of children playing, of cars coming and going.
It's late, and the day will arrive when everything falls away,
but it's taken me this long to really see you,
to know my own depth and breadth,
to surrender to
being.

Winter Sycamore

Once again I go to visit
the tall ancient woman who stands by the river.
It's winter, and her leafless dappled arms
and gnarled fingers reach for cool blue sky,
her shapely torso, wide and welcoming.
She dwells in stillness,
a generous stillness,
and I lean my body against her grizzled skin
to hear her beating heart.
Breathing slowly, we enter timeless space,
embracing and embraced.

How many centuries has she stood here
observing our comings and goings,
how many seasons of budding and birthing
her summertime garment of greenery
before tossing it aside piece by piece
to witness another white winter
in bare bleached bones?

Cardinals whistle and trill in nearby branches,
the river murmurs a litany of old stories
and from far away children's laughter
floats above the treetops. The wise one
keeps her silence as my song weaves its way
through the invisible web uniting us all.

Spirit of the Sundew

Inspired by the painting "Spirit of the Sundew" by Sara Kishwara

This is how it was in ancient times
in a place later known as Earth:
A reverberating stillness.
A marsh asleep in the darkness, waiting.
Black and green Jack's pulpit
and pink mountain laurel
bearing minute water droplets
on trembling skin.
Winged ones, insects, submerged frogs
holding their collective breath
like musicians waiting for the conductor's arrival.
A river of spiny-head vines moving with purpose,
spurring a family of mushrooms to give birth
to the goddess, bodhisattva of the rising sun.
Her deep dream-like meditation,
born of light and water,
radiates a golden orange-green aura
as first flames of dawn emerge behind the pines.
A heron's ragged cry rents the silence
and slowly the goddess dissipates,
leaving behind her a haze
of vernal light and mist.

Silent

The birds are strangely silent this morning.
I hear the wind, weaving through trees.
I hear a faraway murmur from a distant intractable land.

Where are the bright announcements of yesterday's wren,
perched on the shepherd's crook, passionately singing to the
lush amphitheater of yard, to squirrels, chipmunks, and circling hawks?

I suppose there is a time to be silent, when deep listening is called for.
I sit on the deck, breathing through my ears
letting in the vast grace of morning, a rising well of courage
holding right words for the right time.

Visiting Goats

A ride through summer countryside and we
arrive at the goat-lady's home. She emerges
from the garden to greet us, straw hat
circling her head, diffusing yellow light.
She opens up the gateway to the realm
of her beloveds: brown and white Daisy,
Poppy and Blossom–and then there's Ivy,
whose ebony body gleams in the sun.
"Why goats?" we wonder, though we can't deny
their charm. No children here to bring up
on the farm, but lots of room to care for
playful kids who joust 'neath Mother's watchful eye.
Hearts filled with joy and loving nurture
Expand the circle cradling all of nature.

Beach Matter

Inspired by beach refuse collage "the sea is my muse: sea 6" by
Sarah Jane Thornington

Along the shoreline, scanning for bits of treasure,
a chunk of wood tossed and shaped by tides,
surface cracked and sanded as an old fisherman's skin.
And this scrap of bubble-wrap churned up
in the sea foam like sacs of orderly fish eggs.
Artifacts of this time and place,
one acceptable, the other suspect.
Matter that is used to make ships and houses,
hold food and haul trash—
does it matter if it washes up on white beaches?
What is the matter with us if we don't mind
that our refuse compromises our places of refuge?
Hold these materials in your hands—yes there is beauty here,
enough to make a shrine with a clear window
open wide enough to expand perception,
to answer the question:
Does it matter?

The Sorting

I sit on the floor of my studio
at the feet of the old piano
surrounded by a forest
of books and papers,
games for teaching,
precarious stacks and piles.

What do I keep from 36 years
of listening, listening,
pulling on door after door,
finally finding the one
that opens a child's
heart and mind
flooding her with light?

I'll keep the patience they gave me
as I listened to the umpteenth
rendition of "Fur Elise",
as I learned to treasure
each note and stumbled phrase,
celebrate each measure claimed,
receive the gift of joy
as the piece was played
in its entirety,
the player alive with emotion
and confidence—
a new birthing
of being
and Beethoven.

I'll keep their insistence
that I accept them all, as they are,
not bend, coerce, cajole them to my will,
but see who they *really* are—
the keen-eared ones, who can play anything
before I've uttered a word;

the dutiful ones, revealing hidden genius,
if I remember to give them the slightest opening;
the squirmy ones who must *move* their music;
the jokey ones, who get the humor of it;
and the off-beat ones, who might never hear
that steady internal metronome,
but who, nevertheless, play on
with diligence and deep delight,
sometimes for the rest of their lives.

I stand and survey
my accumulated leavings,
worn-out staves and
tattered flashcards.
These papers can go;
I have enough to keep for a lifetime.

At the Airport

In the ladies room
the cleaning woman
scours the sinks.
I greet her and she
returns my hello,
which doesn't always happen.
Often they seem to prefer
to remain anonymous,
invisible.

After I've washed and dried
my hands, without looking up
she says, "Safe travels."
An unexpected blessing.
I want to give her something back,
but all I say, with a light-filled voice is
"Thank you so much."
That is all I can get out.

Yet I want to look her in the eyes,
complete the connection.
Tell her...what?
Have a lovely day?
Thank you for seeing me,
I see you, too.
Thank you for acknowledging
that we both belong
to the same human family,
for not closing yourself off.
Thank you for taking the chance
that you might be ignored,
for keeping your heart open.

For reminding me
it's worth the risk.

Analog Dreams

Living under pale winter sun
makes me crave an analog life—
to spend the day with the solid weight
of a book in my hands, the fireplace blaze

a constant cheering presence.
This day is absent of questions—
so easily answered by the Google-god
who traps me in a mind-stuffing maze

till my brain lights up like an overdone
Christmas tree. Within the snow globe of my world
I gently place a record on the turntable,
let James Taylor fill the room with his fluent tones,

telling me it's gonna be all right, stumbly patches
on a ski run giving way to smooth snowy mounds.
In late afternoon I light some candles,
start the soup, make a meditation of slicing

carrots and onions, sautéing barley in butter,
releasing a flurry of tarragon and thyme into the pot.
I breathe in the fragrance of bliss,
of earthy sustenance my body cries for.

Soon there will be a showy pink and gray sky
in the west, silhouetting the black arms of trees.
I settle into my cozy chair, open a notebook
and write into the winter night.

What You Said

Dark road ahead.
My tires kick up stones,
then settle onto smooth pavement.
The moon emerges from
behind a barn and on cue
a voice beams down—
       your voice.

Whatever our changes, you say,
you can't deny what's true.

I ease into a slow turn.

You have amazing strength,
such an imagination
and rare beauty—inside and out.

The moon glides above the trees;
in seconds I feel the change
written deep in my chest.
A balloon of light fills me,
rises through my head,
out the moon roof,
up and up to join you.
At the last blue moment,
I reach up and catch the string.

The road opens wide
as I bring my
light heart home.

Compliment

I don't mind receiving compliments.
When Laura said she liked the feather design
of my black and white top, it landed well.
I'd gotten past the dowdy, the almost-right for once.

Of course, I know it doesn't mean a thing
but I'll take that boost. It reminds me to
not abandon myself, to stand a little taller,
to wrap myself in a cloak of refracted light,

dragonfly hues of turquoise and emerald.
To enter the room in a state of grace, of belonging,
as do queen bees, monarchs, and even wasps.
Even a mosquito has its moment illuminated by the sun.

Beyond the Border

For Ryan

On the charter from Niantic to Block Island
December sun glints off calm water.
The fishermen lean on the rail,
Watch the cloud-streaked sky,
Anticipate a bountiful catch.

Three hours in, a shift.
The wind changes from caress
To heaving punches, hurling against the tide.
The sea surface ripples into frosty snow
And then comes the first swell—
You can see it in the distance—
A humped sea creature heading right for the boat.

They drop anchor, bow facing the waves,
Ride her up, up, up twelve feet to the top
Then roll all the way
Down down
To a stomach hollowing thump,
Over and over and over—
A carnival ride with no off switch.
The fishermen lean their rods on the rail,
Balancing to stay on board,
Straining every muscle,
Working through nausea.
And the porgy, sea bass, and cod
Seem to leap onto the hooks
As if eager to escape the maelstrom.

Hours later, crossing the Atlantic
Toward home port, the fishermen—
Spent, numb—
Silently watch the sun, low in a hazy sky,
Reflect on calm water.
This short trip has taken them
miles beyond their safe invisible border.
Part of the wall has crumbled.
They carry this awareness home with them.

IV
Women

The Women are Waiting

Inspired by Natalie Van Vleck's painting "Five Women"

They gather here for disparate reasons.
Unspeaking, each slants her head
in a different direction,
listening for instructions
only she can hear. Perhaps a revelation
that makes clear their entire lives
up to this moment.
What sustenance is offered
on this table of longing?
If only it were as easy
as entering this simple room
instead of the inching
loss and gain of their days.
Light the candle, a ritual
that will usher each woman
to her next phase.
In reality, each has visited
many rooms and will inhabit
many more, holding close together
like a stand of trees with mingled roots,
their nascent blooms
trembling in the wind.

One Friday in June

When women were birds, they were free to dip and soar at will.
Then their wings were clipped and they became subject to another's will.

They walked behind the others, allowing themselves to be cared for
as one might care for a beloved pet,

a dog who waits to be fed, or not fed, praised or not, loved or not,
it is out of her control. Walked on a leash, confined
to certain areas of the house, allowed to procreate or not.

A woman might have a lapdog to baby and comfort her
while the wild dog within remains chained in a dark cellar,
becoming more and more desperate.

No wonder she finally broke free to claim her own sovereignty,
to cast votes, own a home, work and claim her own fortune.
To procreate or not, as she chooses.

It took a revolt, a clawing back to basic human rights,
gradual gains leading to victory and rejoicing.

But the others wait at the perimeter for the next chance
to strip them clean, beat them down, return to the past.
Even some of the women are complicit, forgetting their free-flight
before they were earthbound.

It happens on an ordinary day in June.
The pendulum swings, while above,
the birds are watching.

Note: On June 24, 2022, Roe vs. Wade was overturned, ending 50 years of federal
protection of abortion rights.

Regina Laudis

The nuns' church in the woods
could be mistaken for a barn
but when you enter, the faint smell of incense
invades your bones inviting stillness

and it's quiet, so quiet
except for the hum of ceiling fans
twirling like dervishes high in the rafters.

A Christmas tree stands before the altar,
rustic and uneven, no doubt harvested by nuns
from their own cloistered woods,
their strong hands cutting and carrying
while singing a chant by Hildegard in unison.

See what care they took, stringing tiny golden lights,
hanging red balls, paper snowflakes, every sort of bird,
how they lovingly arranged pots of red and white poinsettias
and pink roses around the tree and Baby Jesus,
who lies in a straw-filled manger lined with rabbit fur.

Later, behind the wrought iron gate
that stands between them and the altar,
they will file in and line up
standing face to face
to sing their chants in Latin
and it makes me wonder
what it's like to live exclusively
in the company of women—
like having 30 sisters, each one competing
for attention from their Almighty parents?
Or like water, yeast and flour
blended by alchemy into one body,
one perfect loaf?

They move from milking cows to Third Hour prayer,
shearing sheep to noontime devotions,
stacking cheese to evening Vespers,

working and praying, praying and working,
in celestial rhythm
rocking the world's cradle,
rocking us to peace and sleep.

Ruby, 1925

Thirteen women pose for a photograph
on the steps of a school. Young, bright
and smiling, with stylish bobs and modest skirts,
they seem proud to be teachers,
to be modern, independent women.

You wouldn't guess that underneath their
patterned skirts and long sweaters
they were bound by the tight ropes of a contract
that swore their promise never to be immodest
or unpatriotic, or complain to the school's principal,

never to go dancing,
or fall in love or get secretly married,
to always sleep eight hours each night,
to eat carefully, stay in good spirits,
be willing servants to the school board.

They vowed to cheerfully donate time and money
to Sunday school, to always be a "lady"
and to never attain the advanced age of 41,
at least while so employed. It seemed a better deal
than working in the factory making ball bearings
though teachers' pay was certainly less.

But look at this coterie of women,
how comfortable they seem, how the one in front
with shiny crimped hair and dazzling smile
leans her arm on her friend's knee.

You just know she's the one who'd be
slipping out at night for a movie, bringing girlfriends
to parties with men, jazz and bootleg gin.
These were daring times, after all,
and somehow she knew there were
others right behind her, waves of women
pushing open the heavy door to freedom
one more chink.

Rachel

I'm surprised to see that she is my new physical therapist,
having known her years ago when she was a child and I,
her piano teacher. I remember the smile in her eyes,
the upturned corners and lively spark.

She greets me now with that same brightness—
still Rachel, multiplied by years into necessary womanhood.
I lie on my back and let her talented fingers knead the knots

in my shoulders, coaxing them to relax and melt under her touch.
Her voice, still quiet, but with an added vein of conviction,
as she explains each muscle's function and compiles

a list of exercises for me, much as I had assigned pieces
for her to practice, which she did, faithfully, and
as I recall, with a touch of humor and grace.

I remember her joy when playing Tom Chapin's
version of "Happy Birthday", set to the music
of Franz Lehar's "Merry Widow Waltz".

Her fingers flowed over the keys, sending music
through the air of the retirement home,
a gift of love to her Grandmother Merle.

Happy birthday happy birthday we love you
Happy birthday and may all your dreams come true

Lying here, my life seems like a dream journey through deep woods.
At times the voice of a wise owl draws me forward; other times
I'm halted by a crow's keening or the song of a mockingbird.

What dreams of Rachel's were even now
weaving a future she could touch with her hands
and feel with a knowing heart?

When you blow out the candles, one light stays aglow
It's the love light in your eyes where e'er you go.

I breathe deeply and allow
Rachel's hands to do their work.

Listen to Monk (as sung by Carmen McCrae)

How to explain the deep pleasure
that rises in my belly
when the opening bass line jogs upward
topped off by those three pointy piano chords.
Take a breath for the deep dive
as Carmen effortlessly rides the river
of bass, piano, high hat
with her sublime, earthy voice.
"Thelonius can do that! Listen to this cat!" dat dat daa
She winds through an intricate terrain at pulse-quickening pace
—hairpin turns, loops, figure eights—
then the piano flings its hip story against a jagged mountainside
scaling it up and down,
tosses it to the sax, who weaves it into a dark filigreed forest.
Then the bass, *sotto voce*, each note a ripe plucked berry,
retells all that has been said
in a way it has never been said before.
All the strands converge and
oh baby, we've reached ultimate coherence,
bring it home, Carmen—
"Some cats swing and others don't, Don't you be the kind that won't,
Thelonius can do that! Listen to this cat!" dat dat daaaa

The Supreme Court Rules in Favor of Presidential Immunity

In neighborhoods all over the country
the silent neutrality of trees,
synthesizers of light who
mind the ebb and flow of their lives
while edicts are handed down,
elating the power hungry,
depleting those hungry for justice,
those yearning to breathe free
in their private lives, in their lives
as members of a community,
as citizens of a once free nation,
not naive, not wishing for perfection,
only fairness and adherence
to foundational principles.

We wander streets and forest paths
under the whispering leaves of trees,
hoping to receive instruction
of our interdependence,
a benediction capable of restoring
our individual and collective wellness.
Later, there will be arrows of action,
but for now, this is all we can do,
while our country's brokenness
opens a deep ravine no one can
crawl out of alone. We walk
among the trees and listen
for their wordless wisdom.

V
Spirit

O, my Soul, Come Blend with Me

don't be shy,
no hide-and-seek among the sheets
on the line to dry.
Don't leave me hanging
to navigate this world without
a spirited wind
to fill my sails.
In-spire me, let me breathe you wholly,
fill me with holy fire.
Anoint my eyes,
my ears, my lips.
Bring in clarity.
Bring up courage.
Permeate my cells,
blur my boundaries.
Widen the circumference
of my heart.
Meet me in a whirling womb-space
of ether and air
where we may
mix and merge
in jubilant co-creation.

O my Soul
Come blend with me.

Look Upward

Inspired by J. Neil Bittner's monograph Shutters and Lace

The alley beckons, cool and blue,
shutters in various poses,
letting in the light or denying it.
Eyes are drawn upward to a pair
of juxtaposed balconies, a doorway
flanked by Aegean blue shutters,
dainty lacework hanging at the panes.
Higher still, a small double hung window,
frothy with lace like a hovering angel.
This hidden chapel, wrapped
in the holy hue of the Madonna.
And she, in her secret room,
weaving prayers of beauty
in the morning light.

Solar Light

How to eat the sun:
First, open the top of your head,
let solar light stream in,
suffuse your brain, beam out
from your eyes, ears, mouth.
Swallow it down, gilding your throat
like honey to sweeten your words;
let it stream down your arms
in a rush of liquid photons,
fingertips full enough to send
ten bright rays to kiss the earth.
Let it touch the prism in your heart,
multi-hues to flourish
that inner garden,
enliven your solar plexus,
radiant dazzling orb,
spill into the basin of your belly,
sparking new creations.
Let it flow through each leg,
sweeping away all kinks and creaks
to rest in warm golden slippers on your feet.
Feel the stream in your soles
spread a luminous network
in the Mother's body,
connecting earth and sky
in a nourishing
river of light.

Five Views of a Feather

Inspired by Steve Habersang's pen and ink drawing

A weightless feather
vibrates with infinite love
summoning sparrows

–

The mother has flown.
Released from my origin
I dwell in freedom

–

Let my spine gently
curve to support tensile ribs,
haven for my kin

–

The air breathes through me
spiraling endless circles
of avian song

–

Sustain me, wild sky
until earth draws me downward
in soft enfoldment

Resonance

Five of us in a circle
breathe in and release
soft tones, vibrations rising
in the air like incense.

A sonic *aah* shimmers
before us, a resonant
heart hologram,

original syllable, uttered
to the matrix of our mothers,
the end sound of
Allah and *hallelujah*,

a sound swirling with purpose
and power, expanding our vast
inner chambers with the All
of love.

Fear dissipates, replaced
by gratitude and endless
circles of connection

that hold us close
in the echoing silence
that follows.

Voyage

Sitting in my bedroom chair, I close my eyes
and sense a soft yellow candle flame in my heart,
warming my insides with golden light.

It permeates every cell, radiating outward
until it slips past the boundaries of my body,
continuing on through bright spinning galaxies,
straight into the limitless eye of God.

Suspended, timeless, I am unleashed,
here, yet also there, flesh and spirit,
until the little flame calls me back fully into my body
and I sit bathed in faint, yet certain remembrance
of endless, open possibility.

Liminal

When you come to that place
      in-between
where everything that once made sense
      no longer does,
going forward is not possible.
      Neither is going back.
Exhausted, you lie down right there
      in soft grass
allow your body to surrender completely
      to the body of the Mother.
Stay there until every cell has
agreed and accepted there is
      nothing more to do.

In time, an opening may appear
      distant, foggy.
Give your full focus until
      it reveals
the threshold of an arc that spans
      a liminal river.
You stand on the edge perceiving
      river, hills, sky
as if through a mottled lens.

On the wind, a whiff of a
      new way to be.
It may seem strange. It may be
very different from
      the you of before
yet you know, with long-absent
      certainty:
This is the way forward.
Take one clear step.
The others will follow.

Second Sight

Inspired by Peter Seltzer's pastel Peace That Has No Borders

What is seen and unseen,
not so far apart.
What it takes is a shift in focus.
Use a simple tool, say a frame,
to direct your attention,
clear away everything else
except the pink lotus,
then the blue.

Eventually your two eyes
will tire and close,
drifting your vision upward
to a third frame,
the illuminated template
of "Lotus." Stay with it
and your perception
will widen to include
a magnificent orb
whose energy pulses
beyond the frame.

You may remain in this
timeless state for seconds
or millennia.
Perhaps you become aware
of a being of great compassion
hovering just above your
left shoulder
before you quickly descend
to the safety of red earth
where the framed
pink and blue lotus flowers sit,
right next to a pair of white doves
you never noticed before.

I'm in a New Place, She Said

For the singing goddesses

How did it happen?
A rolling ride on wings of grace
spiraling through ascending forests.
Then, expansive view, uncluttered,
blessed with gliding birds and clear vision,
the wind's song in my ears,
its bright rise and fall
zinging through my cells.
And here you are in the swirl
of fresh sounds, shapes, colors,
voices blending, angelic.
Holding gratitude for the muddied path
that brought us here, the holy journey
both arduous and effortless,
our song flowing in deep streams
of numinous light

Acknowledgements

My deep gratitude goes to Sandy Carlson and Ed Dzitko, founders of Orenaug Mountain Publishing, for their constant support and encouragement.

Sandy, thank you for opening the door wide for me to return to my poetry roots.

Members of the Orenaug Mountain poetry group, your enthusiasm, support and feedback add such joy to my life.

About the Author

Julia Cook is a lifelong lover and writer of poetry from an early age. For many years, her poems were a private way of marking the events and emotions of her life. Gradually she began to share them with family and friends, and to convert some into lyrics for original choral compositions.

Julia facilitates classes on poetry, writing, and music at the Osher Lifelong Learning Institute at the University of Connecticut, Waterbury.

She has published poems in the Orenaug Mountain anthologies (*The Harvest and the Reaping, Winter Glimmerings, Whose Spirits Touch, We Are Here, Personal Freedom, From Art to Art, The Nature of Woodbury, Instances of Seeing* and *Instances of Seeing, Volume II*) and the online Orenaug Mountain Poetry Journal.

Additionally, her work has appeared in the Osher Lifelong Learning Institute newsletter and on the website of Music for People.

This is her first book of poetry.

About Orenaug Mountain Publishing (OMP)

It is the vision of Orenaug Mountain Publishing (www.orenaugmountainpublishing.com) to be a beacon for poetic expression and to create a platform for poets to share their work with the world.

We seek to champion the art of poetry of writers around the world by publishing high-quality work that challenges, inspires, and connects readers to the human experience.

We do this through several themed anthology projects a year and via the online Orenaug Mountain Poetry Journal at www.orenaugmountainpoetry.net.

Visit our website to learn more about what we do, and to find out how to take part in our anthologies or our poetry journal.

www.ingramcontent.com/pod-product-compliance
Lightning Source LLC
Chambersburg PA
CBHW050906100426
42737CB00048B/3219